"I absolutely loved Pam's use of the 'paradise' of Louisiana to herald the *Paradise* that comes from knowing Jesus and His grace. I heartily recommend her book! It will lead you to the grace of God and hopefully encourage you to visit Louisiana."

Frank Friedmann
Teaching pastor, Grace Life Fellowship

"For all who know and love Louisiana, there are familiar surroundings that declare God's glory and grace...if one will simply look. In *Lagniappe upon Lagniappe*, Pam Braud gives us a beautiful and inspiring glimpse, through this place that we love, of the Person Who loves us so much. Your heart will be captivated not only because you love where you live, but especially because of the One Who loves where He lives...in you!"

Tim Chalas
Lead pastor, Grace Life Fellowship

"*Lagniappe* was very inspiring to me! I enjoyed seeing His life revealed in my own backyard and considering how Jesus ministers life to whomever, wherever. This book encouraged me with its completely unique and creative take on Louisiana! Thanks, Pam, for being obedient to write as God inspired you!"

Jennie Seals
Retired flight attendant
now a flight attendant for the Heaven-Bound, Hospice Specialist

"The exotic backdrop of South Louisiana frames insightful spiritual meditations on God's grace and mercy. This may become a Louisiana classic!"

Devera Goss
Nurse and hospice worker

"Enthralled! The stories are like home to me. Some are familiar and others are pleasant surprises, all inviting us to listen and know our Creator and Father's intentions for us."

Dawn Theriot
A bayou local

"A genre all its own, combining Louisiana culture and spiritual insight. You can't wait to read the next page."

Roberta Schroeder
Office manager, Grace Life Fellowship

"A great read, blending the deep truths of Christ's love for us with a tour through the rich culture of Louisiana. Whether you were born and raised in Louisiana or simply love learning about our rich heritage, Pam presents a great concept—Christ's parables as if He were telling them to a group of Cajuns. Like the perfect gumbo, the ingredients of timeless biblical truth mixed with the unique seasonings of Louisiana's history and culture make for a great read. So get a cup of coffee, grab some beignets, sit in your comfortable reading chair, and enjoy!"

Bob Seals, Jr.
Retired bank executive

Lagniappe upon Lagniappe:

Grace Parables of South Louisiana

By Pam Musso Braud

Scripture quotations taken from the New American Standard Bible® (NASB). Copyright © 1960, 1962, 1963, 1968, 1971, 1972, 1973, 1975, 1977, 1995 by The Lockman Foundation.
Used by permission. www.Lockman.org

© 2017 Pam Musso Braud All rights reserved.

Lazarus Media Productions.

ISBN 978-1542656993

2018-2019

For those who love Louisiana

July 4, 2019

Mom,

I know you love Louisiana and you love God! This little book will remind you of so much you know about both, and some ways they are related. Enjoy!

Love,
Dianne

Contents

Acknowledgment • 10

Introduction • 11

Le Père Indien • 15

Longfellow's Lovers • 18

Term of Endearment • 24

Atchafalaya Adventure • 28

Don't Settle for a Shadow • 33

Félicité, "Angel of Mercy" • 38

Cisterns • 41

Mardi Gras Masks • 46

Maw Maw's Trivet • 50

The Life of a Sugar Cane Stalk • 54

The Miracle Water of Abita Springs • 58

Marrow and Fatness • 61

"Lost" Bread • 65

The Better Part • 68

The Exotic Invader • 73

In the Eye of the Storm • 76

The Spiderweb Wedding • 79

Lagniappe • 84

A Note to the Reader • 88

"For of His fullness we have all received,
and grace upon grace."
John 1:16

Acknowledgment

I gratefully acknowledge the teaching of Frank Friedmann, who introduced me to the New Covenant of Jesus Christ. Thank you, Frank, for your faithfulness to the gospel.

I am also indebted to Josh Gordon and the staff of *Lazarus Media Productions* for their patient assistance throughout the publication process.

And thank you to family and friends who told me to just write and quit talking about it. I love you for that. I especially appreciate my husband Craig's valuable input and steadfast encouragement, even when I whined.

Introduction

I wrote this little book because I love God and I love Louisiana. It's that simple. I see His hands all over her narratives. And I see elements of her story as object lessons of His own great story, the redemption of humanity. As I've continued to explore Louisiana, she has offered me striking visual aids of God's love and grace, and I want to share them with you.

My re-discovery of Louisiana began a few years ago, when I became intrigued by the Apostle Paul's use of particular cultural references in his presentation of the gospel message. According to the book of Acts, he preached to the people of Athens using examples from their own society. As he walked around the city, the apostle was grieved by the city's culture of idol worship, and he addressed a crowd who wanted to hear more about Jesus and the resurrection. Standing in the Areopagus (the meeting place of the Athenian court), Paul said:

> The God who made the world and all things in it… made from one man every nation of mankind to live on all the face of the earth… He is not far from each one of us; for in Him we live and move and exist, as even some of your own poets have said, *'For we also are his children.'* Being then the children of God, we ought not to think that the Divine Nature is like gold or silver or stone, an image formed by the art and thought of man…God is now declaring to men that all people everywhere

should repent, because He has fixed a day in which He will judge the world in righteousness through a Man whom He has appointed, having furnished proof to all men by raising Him from the dead. (Acts 17:24-31, emphasis mine).

Paul Preaching in Athens, by Raphael, 1515

In presenting the gospel to the people of Athens, Paul had options. He could have quoted words Jesus spoke about Himself during His time on earth. Or he could have cited Old Testament verses that prophesied the Messiah. Instead, led by the Holy Spirit, the apostle chose to begin his message by quoting the writings of a pagan poet (the modern equivalent would be quoting lyrics from a pop song). Paul began with a kernel of truth that was familiar to his listeners and from there launched a biblical presentation about the nature of God

Introduction

and His salvation. He started with a cultural reference well known to his listeners, and he ended with the gospel.

Of course, Jesus had already set the standard for the use of cultural allusions in teaching. As He depended upon His Father for words to communicate with people, the Holy Spirit often led Jesus to teach using object lessons based on everyday life in Israel. The gospels are filled with His stories about business, government, wedding customs, athletic events, war, and geography of that time period. He used ordinary items, such as salt, light, moths, rust, lilies, dogs, fish, sheep, vineyards, water, mud, seeds, fields, pearls, bread, camels, fig trees, yokes, and stones to illustrate truth.

The writers of the epistles, also inspired by the Holy Spirit, did the same thing. They evoked common images from nature, such as the grafting of branches, the leavening of dough, thorns, sowing and reaping, and heavenly bodies. They used familiar legal references in the epistles—slavery, chains, freedom, adoption, inheritance, ambassadorship, and legal wills. They wrote of architecture, athletics, seafaring, and war; they used metaphors dealing with the human body and musical instruments.

As I thought about these ideas, I began to wonder how particular aspects of Louisiana's culture might illustrate God's grace and truth found in Christ. What natural, historical, or cultural features of Louisiana could Jesus or Paul have used as a starting point to tell the Good News of the gospel? What "parables" could He have told in the Bayou State?

This little book touches on only a small portion of what Louisiana proclaims about God's grace and truth. I hope as you read it and consider the Bible verses following each chapter, you will be increasingly astounded at the love and grace of God. I also hope you will see our state's uniqueness as Father's gift to us. May we appreciate our home in Louisiana all the more for what it reveals to us of the Creator, who offers life through Jesus Christ, until such time as our home is finally and forever in heaven with Him.

Pam Braud
Baton Rouge, Louisiana
March 2017

Le Père Indien

In 1753, Louisiana was governed by the French Marquis de Vaudreuil, but it was home to many tribes of Native Americans, among them the Colapissa and Choctaw tribes. One day a Choctaw man insulted a Colapissa by saying that his tribesmen were "dogs" (slaves) of the French. The offended Colapissa happened to be holding a loaded musket in his hand, and in his anger he fired it at the Choctaw. When he realized what he had done, he fled to New Orleans.

After the wounded Choctaw died, his family went to New Orleans and demanded of Governor Vaudreuil the surrender of the Colapissa murderer. The marquis tried to appease the Choctaw man's relatives with gifts, but the family refused to be placated with anything less than a life for a life. Finally, Vaudreuil sent orders to the commandant of the French post to capture the guilty man. By this time, however, the killer had fled to the German Coast and no one could find him.

To preserve peace, the aged father of the killer stepped forward and offered to give his own life to the Choctaws in payment for the crime of his son. The family of the deceased agreed to accept the noble sacrifice of the murderer's father. The old Colapissa stretched himself out on the trunk of a tree, and a Choctaw warrior severed his head from his body with one stroke.

Choctaw Village near the Chefuncte, by Francois Bernard, 1869,
Peabody Museum, Harvard University

Governor Vaudreuil's wife, a patron of the arts who regularly hosted musical and theatrical receptions and festivities, found this story so moving that she commissioned LeBlanc de Villeneuve, a French military officer stationed in New Orleans, to write a play about it. The play was titled *Le Père Indien*. It was the first drama of native origin enacted in what is now the United States. Unfortunately, the play was lost; as far as we know, it was never printed, and no copy is known to exist. Early historians of Louisiana have preserved the story for us.

This incredible account of a father's sacrifice on behalf of his guilty child gives us a picture, though imperfect, of our own heavenly Father's tender mercy toward us.

Related Verses:
- John 3:16
- Romans 5:8
- Romans 8:39
- Titus 3:4-7

Longfellow's Lovers

Louisiana claims as its own two of the most tragic lovers in American history. The backdrop of Evangeline and Gabriel's story was the 18th century struggle between the French and the British for control of Canada.

In 1755, the British government of Nova Scotia expelled the French Acadian settlers who had farmed the area for over a hundred years. Not only did the British ship the Frenchmen to ports in England and France and along the east coast of the United States, but they also cruelly placed family members on different vessels so that relatives could not reunite. Many of the Acadian outcasts eventually found their way to Louisiana's swamps and bayous, where there was already a well-established French community.

In Massachusetts in 1840, nearly a century after the expulsion of the Acadians from Canada, Henry Wadsworth Longfellow hosted a dinner party attended by Nathaniel Hawthorne and a clergyman friend of Hawthorne's. The pastor recounted a story that a churchgoer had told him about a betrothed Acadian couple who were to have been married in 1755. Sadly, the wedding was to have taken place on the same day that the great Acadian exile, or *le grand dérangement*, occurred. The marriage, of course, could not transpire, and Gabriel was one of those deported by the British, leaving behind the heartbroken Evangeline.

Longfellow became very interested in the couple's sad story, and he eventually adapted it into his epic poem, *Evangeline*. The long poem about the lovers was immensely successful. It so popularized the characters of Evangeline and Gabriel that school children all over the United States were assigned to memorize parts of the work. In the 1920s, silent film actress Dolores del Río played the lead in Hollywood's adaptation of Evangeline's story. Del Río later posed for the statue of Evangeline shown on page 23, located in St. Martinville. A local young woman was even selected as "Queen Evangeline."

Henry Wadsworth Longfellow

In Longfellow's version of the story, Evangeline searches high and low all over the United States for her lost love. Finally, after many years of vainly tracking him, she enters a convent. In a Philadelphia hospital, she recognizes Gabriel on his deathbed. Her final words are thanks to God for having given her a last chance to see her beloved. A Louisiana edition of the tale has the lovers reuniting under an oak tree on the banks of the Bayou Teche, near present-day St. Martinville, where Evangeline learns that Gabriel now belongs to someone else. In this version, she is grief-stricken and dies an insane woman.

To modern readers, Evangeline may seem like a very melodramatic heroine. But for me, she effectively illustrates the truth that love can compel a lover to extreme or seemingly illogical actions. Evangeline simply refused to imagine life without her beloved. Consider the extreme action of God the Father, as the Supreme Lover, on our behalf.

In response to our sin, even though we had forsaken Him, He sent His Son to pursue us to earth, pay for our sins, and restore us to His arms of love and intimacy.

The story of Evangeline and Gabriel also poses the question of the nature of truth. What is truth, and what is illusion? At one point in Longfellow's poem, a priest encourages Evangeline to trust in what she knows in her heart, even though she cannot see it—that her beloved Gabriel truly is near. Other characters in the story label as illusion Evangeline's faith in a reunion with Gabriel, but the priest tells her:

> Therefore trust to thy heart, and to what the world
>   calls illusions.
> Gabriel truly is near thee; for not far away to the
>   southward,
> On the banks of the Teche are the towns of St.
>   Maur and St. Martin.

In reality, people do sometimes look at what is true and think it is an illusion. Have you ever been labeled naïve or idealistic because of your faith in Christ? If so, don't be discouraged—in the words of Longfellow's priest to Evangeline, Jesus "is truly near thee." Jesus is the truth, though some do not accept Him as such.

Longfellow's cleric also utters words that ring true for Christians, who are journeying toward our meeting with our divine Lover, Jesus: "There the long-wandering bride shall be given again to her bridegroom, There the long-absent pastor regain his flock and his sheepfold."

Through the cross of the Great Shepherd, God has regained His flock. The long-wandering bride—those who believe in Christ—will one day be given to her Bridegroom. If we have trusted Christ, then

Evangeline Discovering Her Affianced in the Hospital, by Samuel G. Richards, circa 1889, Detroit Institute of Arts

we have been restored to God, and one day we will meet Him face to face. That is good news, not an illusion!

The name of Longfellow's heroine—Evangeline—means "messenger of good news." The gospel of Jesus brought us the good news of redemption and of life in our Savior. It's the invitation to know, as Paul prayed for the Ephesians, the breadth and length and height and depth of the love of Christ. It's also our reason to celebrate a Beloved whose demonstrated commitment to us far surpasses that of any human lover.

Trust His heart toward you, for it is so good that He searched for you because He refused to imagine life without you!

Related Verses:

1 Corinthians 2:8-10

2 Corinthians 5:7

Ephesians 3:14-19

Luke 19:10

Matthew 13:44-46

Hebrews 11:6

Evangeline, by Edwin Douglas

Bronze statue atop the empty tomb of Evangeline in St. Martinville, sculpted by Marcelle Rebecchini. The statue was dedicated in 1931 by Mexican actress Dolores del Río, who played the role of Evangeline in Hollywood's version of the story and also served as the model for the monument.

Term of Endearment

We southerners are known for our use of affectionate nicknames. If you live in Louisiana you've probably known someone called Bubba, Sis, Boo, or Bee. But in the southern part of Louisiana you might also hear another term of endearment—the word *cher*.

Cher (or the feminine form *chère*) came to Louisiana via the Acadians. Referring to someone as *cher* (pronounced "sha" as in "shack," without the final consonant) is like saying "dear" or "darling." It expresses that the addressee is precious or beloved. For example, a grandparent might call to a small child, "Come here, *cher*, and give me a hug!" You can also hear the word *cher* in the lyrics of many Cajun love songs.

Cher can also refer to someone who is not necessarily a close relative or friend but who is still very much appreciated. If you are leaving a retail store after paying for an item and the clerk tells you, "Thanks for shopping with us, *cher*," it's a good-natured sign of gratitude for your business.

The word *cher* originated with the French verb *chérir*, meaning to cherish. It is related to a Latin word signifying "beloved," "high-priced," or "costly" and usually implies tenderness, protectiveness, acceptance, and some level of connection or intimacy. It signifies that you in some way share life with that person.

Even though the apostle Paul never used the word *cher*—the French language wouldn't be developed for a few more centuries—we see in his epistles that he esteemed personal relationships. One example is in his letter to the Thessalonians. His involvement with the believers in Thessalonica went deeper than the words he spoke to them while present among them. He wasn't a "hit-and-run" evangelist, too busy for authentic, intimate connection. I believe Paul would have enjoyed using the word *cher*, had he been familiar with it, to describe his feelings for the Thessalonian Christians. He was protective over and concerned for the welfare of these beloved believers. You could say that the church there was very *cher* to him. He used a term meaning much the same thing as *cher* in his first letter to the Thessalonians. He wrote in 1 Thessalonians 2:7-8:

> But we proved to be gentle among you, as a nursing mother tenderly *cares for* her own children. Having so fond an affection for you, we were well-pleased to impart to you not only the gospel of God but also our own lives, because you had become very dear to us (emphasis mine).

Not only had Paul shared the gospel with the Thessalonians, but he had also come to cherish them. The Greek word translated as "cares for" means "to soften by heat" and was used of a mother bird spreading her feathers around her chicks to keep them warm. The idea the apostle presents is his parental care and tender affection toward the Thessalonians, qualities that had their source in Jesus Christ.

Paul's words remind us of Jesus' expressed desire to care for Israel in Matthew 23:37, where He lamented over the people of Jerusalem,

"How often I wanted to gather your children together, the way a hen gathers her chicks under her wings, and you were unwilling."

According to 1 John 4:19, "We love, because He first loved us." The love that Paul displayed toward those he mentored originated in the Father, who chose to hold us dear and cherish us. Mutual sharing of life, the use of terms of endearment, and the enjoyment of the beloved's affection—these are what characterize life with Jesus.

Matthew 19:13-15 tells of a group of children whom Jesus gathered and held close to Himself. Had He spoken Cajun French, would He have used the term *cher* to tenderly call these little ones to come and enjoy sitting with Him? Perhaps He would even have used the common Cajun term *cher bébé*. I am certain that whatever He said, His words inspired in his listeners the same sense of closeness and security that the word *cher* does for me.

Term of Endearment

Cher is a great term to describe the way our Father feels about His children. He is my *cher* and I am His. Our lives are intertwined. Nothing can separate me from the warmth of His love. My ability to cherish Him is simply my response to the way He treasures me.

Imagine Jesus whispering to you, "*Cher*, live from Me! I cherish you more than you know. You are so dear to me. Receive from Me all day long. Let's live life together as you abide in Me!"

Related Verses:

1 Peter 2:3-5

Ephesians 2:3-5

2 Thessalonians 2:16-17

1 John 4:19

Atchafalaya Adventure

You haven't really experienced Louisiana until you've spent a night or two with family or friends on a houseboat in the swamp. I've had two such weekend adventures in the Atchafalaya Basin, with the little red houseboat we rented tied up to a cypress stump in a small bayou.

Atchafalaya Adventure

The vast Atchafalaya Basin has always appeared beautiful to me in a primeval sort of way. Our little group watched elegant water birds, such as blue herons and snowy egrets, soar above the boat, then gracefully land to wade in the shallow water on the edge of the bayou. We scanned fallen trees and mud banks along the bayou looking for

alligators we knew could see us, but it was autumn, when the great reptiles begin to slow down and don't sun themselves as much. A couple of us made a little fishing expedition in a small *bateau*, which was fun but resulted only in frustrated efforts to catch the garfish that we could see but never hook. We stargazed, away from the lights of "civilization," and we listened to the loud night calls of owls and beavers. One night we even faced a severe thunderstorm on the water, lamentably with no access to cable or online weather reports, when the boat rocked and pulled against its mooring.

My visits to the Atchafalaya Basin were deliberate ventures into that environment, and they were unique and enjoyable trips with loved ones. But as lovely as it is, the swamp is also a bit forbidding. If I had been out in those wetlands alone, I'm certain I would have found the Basin to be a terrifying place.

I wonder how Jesus felt when the Holy Spirit led Him into the desert after John had baptized Him in the Jordan River. After such a momentous event, He spent forty days in the wilderness, tempted by Satan, who continually tried to seduce Him to choose to act independently of His Father's power and direction, to live for the pleasures of life in this world, and to cede authority to him. In addition to the stress of constant temptation, Jesus probably would also have faced the threat of wild beasts, hunger, thirst, and exposure to the elements.

I wonder as well if the Father might have encouraged Jesus with the memory of His recent baptism. Perhaps Jesus remembered the appearance of the dove as it descended from the bright sky, flitting nearer and nearer to Him. I wonder if He recalled the pressure of the dove's talons as it came to rest on Him, or the coolness of river water on His skin. Did He play over and over in his mind the announcement of His Father's voice from heaven, "You are My beloved Son, in You I am well-pleased"? Did these thoughts provide Him with a "hug" from His Abba, an affirmation of His identity as the Pleasing One?

How could Jesus survive such an intense, lengthy trial? True, He was simultaneously 100% man and 100% God. However, if He had used His deity to endure the wilderness, then we would have no hope

Angels Ministering to Christ in the Desert, by Thomas Cole, 1843

of getting through trials, because we are not deity. Jesus had to depend upon His Father, moment by moment, for strength and direction.

Let it comfort us to know that when we go through a trial, our Father will customize His encouragement to us. He is intimately aware of all our needs, and He acts personally and uniquely with relation to us. He offers Himself as our Deliverer in each difficult situation, even as He urges us to the end of our own resources so that we might live from His inexhaustible ones. In the midst of our own personal wilderness, we can know Him as never before.

A weekend in the swampy wilderness may be out of your comfort zone, but if you do brave such a trip, think of Jesus, who walked right into the wilderness, outside of the security of civilization, and personally experienced the deliverance of His Father in the midst of temptation and physical deprivation.

Related Verses:

Mark 1:9-13

2 Corinthians 7:5-6

Romans 8:35-39

Isaiah 33:6

John 10:27-30

Don't Settle for a Shadow

One of Louisiana's most photographed plantation homes is The Shadows-on-the-Teche, situated on the banks of the serene Bayou Teche in New Iberia. Growing up in that town, I daily passed in front of the majestic antebellum home and was told that my grandmother had attended parties there in the 1920s, when the home was still in the hands of a descendant of the original builder. She and fellow partygoers floated down the bayou in canoes, singing and strumming their ukeleles. Of course, I visited The Shadows myself both as a schoolgirl and as an adult. The site is an imposing finale to a long line of lovely old mansions along the highway into town, and it is an anchor both to Main Street and to my childhood.

Constructed in New Iberia in the 1830s by sugar grower David Weeks, The Shadows was supposedly named by Weeks' granddaughter. It was an apt name for a setting eclipsed by the live oak trees around the residence. Unfortunately, David Weeks died before he could occupy his new home, but his widow Mary moved into the house with their large family. Mary died in her sleep there in 1863 as Union troops occupied the plantation. David and Mary Weeks' great-grandson, William Weeks Hall, restored The Shadows in the 1920s and bequeathed it to the National Trust for Historic Preservation

The Shadows-on-the-Teche, National Trust Historic Site,
New Iberia, Louisiana

(www.shadowsontheteche.org). Today tourists stroll under those old oaks, which now cast much greater shadows than they did in the 1800s.

Shadows have always been a source of mystery and romantic inspiration. Virgil, Homer, Shakespeare, and Tennyson all utilized the image of the shadow, and many ancient proverbs speak of them. Robert Louis Stevenson penned the familiar line, "I have a little shadow that goes in and out with me," at about the same time that The Shadows-on-the-Teche was given its name.

But I personally never gave much thought to the significance of shadows until I began to study the use of the shadow image in the New Testament. The apostle Paul spoke of the Old Covenant regulations regarding diet and offerings and festivals as "a mere shadow of what is to come." The writer of Hebrews said that the Law is only a "shadow of the good things to come and not the very form of things."

These verses prompt the question, what did the New Testament writer mean by "the good things to come"? And what did the Law foreshadow? This is an important issue, because if there is something better than a system of righteousness based on keeping the Ten Commandments and other laws, don't we want to know about it?

Paul taught that the "good things to come" refers to the New Covenant, which began at the cross. At the cross of Christ, the believer died with Jesus, was buried with Him, and then was raised as a new creature filled with Jesus' resurrection life. The Old Covenant was just a shadow of this new economy that God brought about through Jesus. The new and better covenant focuses on our resurrection to new life in

Shadows-on-the-Teche, Bayou Side View, by Marie Adrien Persac, 1861

Christ. In this system Christ expresses His own holy life through us. Law keeping is far inferior because it can't ever make us holy.

The Bible teaches that the Law was never meant to be a rulebook for holy living. Once it showed us that we needed Christ, its purpose in our lives ended. The law has no life to impart. The substance of the Christian life is Jesus, and once we are in a relationship with Him, our relationship with the Law is over.

Shadows have a scientific cause. The shadow of a tree is only an image of the real tree, not the real thing. If we settle for a shadow—keeping the Law—we won't enjoy the real thing—Jesus living His life in us and through us by faith.

Shakespeare wrote, "Some there be that shadows kiss; such have but a shadow's bliss." We can enjoy only the shadow of the real thing if we try to live by the Ten Commandments or by any other set of principles. God wants so much more for us than a life lived by a regimen of rules. Spiritual life is found only in Jesus.

Related Verses:

Colossians 2:16-17

Hebrews 8:4-5

Galatians 3:24-25

Romans 3:20

Acts 13:39

Hebrews 10:1

Don't Settle for a Shadow

Félicité, "Angel of Mercy"

In 1839, the town of New Iberia fell prey to a devastating yellow fever epidemic. Nearly half of the community of 500 citizens died. Although we know today that the mosquito *Aedes aegypti* carries the virus that causes the disease, at that time no one knew the real cause of yellow fever, and it was believed to be highly contagious. Those who tended the sick and dying had to wonder if they might be the next to succumb to "yellow jack."

In the late 19th century, Louisiana historian William Henry Perrin wrote about the 1839 epidemic. In his account, he made particular note of an older black woman named Félicité, a native of Santo Domingo, who was immune to the virus. In his *History of Iberia Parish, Louisiana*, Perrin praised her courage and compassion:

> She did an angel's part…She nursed the sick, administered to the dying, closed the eyes of the dead, and wept over their graves. From that year (1839) to the time of her death she was never forgotten or allowed to want by the sufferers of that dreadful period. Her picture adorned the parlors of a number of her white friends, and annually, on the 1st of January, many substantial tokens of the love and friendship they cherished for her found their way to her humble cabin. The day of her death, in February, 1852, was one of general mourning in New Iberia. By common request her body lay in state in the home of her former owner. The funeral rites

were of the most solemn and imposing character. Every business house in New Iberia was closed, and every man, woman and child in the town followed her to the last resting place.

Félicité's ministry to the sick and dying of New Iberia seems to have been completely voluntary and filled with mercy. Her kindness broke racial barriers of the time, and the townspeople decided that her name should not "drop into oblivion." Today a Louisiana state historical marker in her honor stands near New Iberia's city hall.

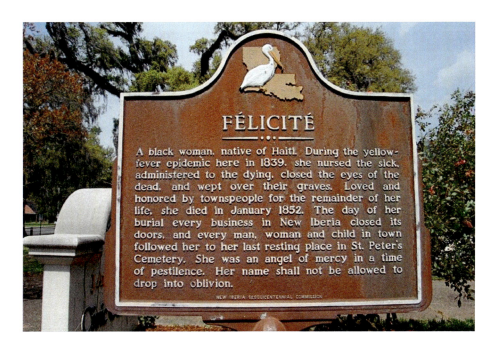

History does not record Félicité's faith, so we don't know if her service to others was spiritually motivated. But her story does remind us that love involves a choice. The perfect example of such love is Jesus, who chose to die upon a cross for us. If Jesus lives in us, then we are also home to His love, a love that we can express to others through faith in Him.

Related Verses:

    Galatians 5:1, 13-16

    1 Peter 2:16

    1 John 3:18

    Colossians 3:12

    John 13: 34

    Romans 5:6-8

Cisterns

When I was growing up in south Louisiana, my family enjoyed visiting my aunt and uncle's fishing camp on Lake Verret. The camp was accessible only by a three-minute boat ride from Attakapas Landing, so to me it was located in the wilderness. Nevertheless, it did have a water supply, thanks to a large wood cistern that collected rainwater. The cistern was painted red and black like a checkerboard (hence, my uncle's nickname Checkerboard)—and when we crossed Lake Verret approaching the shoreline where the camp stood, I watched for the colorful landmark that sat by the building. My family was thankful that we did not have to transport our own supply of water for drinking, cooking, and bathing.

Naturally, the cistern water we used on these visits was purified. But Louisianans have not always had the luxury of clean drinking water. In the early 19th century, fewer than a hundred miles to the east of Lake Verret, the growing city of New Orleans struggled with the issue of water supply. Only the wealthy could avail themselves of the very primitive and expensive subscription-only water works, a system that used hollowed-out cypress logs to carry unpurified water drawn from the Mississippi River. The water was pumped by slave labor into a reservoir. In 1850, health officials declared the supply of drinking water in the city inadequate, stating, "It is painful to reflect upon the frequent sufferings of the working classes for the want of an abundance of pure water." During droughts water had to be hauled from the river at personal cost and purified at the individual's initiative, usually with alum.

Eventually, people began to build cypress cisterns to collect and store rainwater. Gardner's *New Orleans Directory for 1861* lists 35 cistern makers in that city (for a population of nearly 170,000) as well as five companies that manufactured cisterns. In 1892, the entire city depended upon these tanks for its water supply. The cistern industry was international as well: at one time, New Orleans furnished most of the cisterns used in Central America and Mexico.

In 1900, however, the *Aedes aegypti* mosquito was proved to be the cause of yellow fever, and cisterns immediately began to fall out of favor with health officials. A commentator in New Orleans welcomed the implementing of a new water supply system in 1909, saying that the cistern "is the home and the breeding place of the yellow fever mosquito and has been the cause of propagating and spreading the plague. Thousands of lives have been sacrificed in this city to the cistern system, and it will always be a terrible menace to the public health."

Besides posing threats to public health, cisterns are imperfect containers for water because, in spite of the durability of cypress, they develop cracks and holes. In an interesting

Aedes aegypti

CISTERNS

A NEW ORLEANS YARD AND CISTERN.

Illustration from Eliza Ripley's *Social Life in Old New Orleans*, 1912

verse in the book of Jeremiah, God reproached His people for their self-sufficiency. They chose, He said, to construct leaky, untrustworthy cisterns of impure water rather than trust in His constant provision of living water. They rejected the fountain of fresh water for a man-made tank filled with chinks and crevices.

Jesus offers us the same effervescing water that the Israelites rejected. Now, under the New Covenant inaugurated at Jesus' death, the vessels of living water are you and I. He proclaims, "If anyone is thirsty, let him come to Me and drink. He who believes in Me, as the Scripture said, 'From his innermost being will flow rivers of living water.'" Why should we build a cistern to supply us with whatever we think we need for life, when we have this river of living water, God's Holy Spirit dwelling in us? God is the true thirst slayer. Nothing else will satisfy us but His living water.

Cypress cisterns are rarely seen today except as relics of the past. The next time you see one near an old house, remember the fountain of living water that Jesus offers us.

> Shall a cistern hold my heart
> Which cracks and leaks and falls apart?
> It holds no water, slays no thirst.
> Why would my soul pursue it first?
>
> Christ is the fountain flowing ever,
> River of life, now and forever,
> Living water, refreshment pure,
> Cascade that my life secures.
>
> I have sipped from many cisterns
> Tasted many waters bitter.

But not a draft would I repeat,
My satisfaction is complete.

Drink, o saint—drink long and deep!
His well is full, His water sweet.
The Spirit pours from deep within
No cistern can compare with Him.

Related Verses:

    Jeremiah 2:13

    John 4:13-14

    John 7:38

    Revelation 21:6

    Psalm 36:8

Home with cistern in Schriever, Louisiana

Mardi Gras Masks

The last day before the beginning of the Lenten season is known in many churches in Louisiana as Shrove Tuesday, Fat Tuesday, or Mardi Gras. It is the last "bash" before a period of about six weeks of solemnity leading up to the celebration of the resurrection of Jesus Christ at Easter. The commemoration of Mardi Gras is a popular tradition in many parts of Louisiana besides New Orleans. Festivities include parades with all kinds of "throws" and galas with spectacularly costumed revelers.

One feature of the season's holiday dress is the Mardi Gras mask. Masks may take various shapes, but they generally cover the top half of the face, with slits for the eyes, and are decorated with bright colors and feathers or sequins. The purpose of the mask is to conceal the identity of its wearer, mostly just for fun, but in some cases allowing the person to act as he or she wishes without consequence.

Though the use of masks goes back to pagan times, masks have actually been around since the first humans inhabited the Garden of Eden. After Adam and Eve sinned, they clothed themselves with fig leaves, and although these weren't worn on the face, they comprised a type of mask: the first two humans were trying to conceal the shame that sin had created. They wanted to hide from God and from each other.

Disguise goes on today, even in the church. We are afraid to let others see us for who we are. We feel that somehow we just don't measure up to the Christian "benchmark." Such standards are what

Jesus has set us free from. When we walk in His Spirit in rest and in freedom from law—whether that law is self-induced or imposed by other people—we are able to live without a mask. We don't have to hide, because we are totally and completely accepted in Christ!

The following is an imaginary invitation from Jesus to you, asking you to allow Him to remove any self-protective mask that you might be wearing. Prayerfully consider its message. And when you see Mardi Gras partygoers masquerading behind their colorful masks, thank Him that you do not have to conceal yourself, flaws and all, from Him or from anyone else, because He has made you acceptable forever through the cross.

I am the mask remover. I am the one Person who can remove the makeshift face you wear, the fig leaves of your soul. When you look in the mirror, your mask tells you that you need it to survive, that you are not acceptable without it. There is nothing further from My truth. Remember, I myself have made you acceptable through my blood. As a child of God, you are and always will be completely accepted by Me. I see you beneath your disguises, and I see a new creation.

As you abide in Me, I will gently remove the mask behind which you hide. You can then become the vessel of My life and love to needy humanity, who live behind their own masks. You will bear the sweet aroma of My life to those who want to be saved from sin and self. The truth is that you, My child, wear My glory. Why would you want to mask it? You settle for second best when you hide in fear.

Give Me your permission to remove your mask. I have already clothed you with My righteousness. Would you put a mask over the face of a beautiful newborn child? That is how I see you—as My own child, bearing My image and reflecting My glory.

Related Verses:

Genesis 3:6-8

Romans 8:1-2

2 Corinthians 2:14

1 John 3:1

2 Corinthians 3:18

Maw Maw's Trivet

Some of my most enduring memories are of visits to my grandparents' home in Thibodaux, Louisiana. When I was young, they lived in a large two-storied wooden house on Jackson Street, with a wide front porch, from which we grandchildren watched many Mardi Gras and Firemen's Festival parades. Some weekends we just sat on the front steps and visited with each other, or we waited for 18-wheelers to rumble by as they left Highway 1 headed for Highway 90, so that we could signal to them to honk their great horns.

The porch was a fun place, but the part of my grandparents' house that I longed to visit most was, of course, the one place I did not have permission to play. The upstairs couldn't have been more attractive if it had been a castle tower. The uninhabited second story was practically unvisited and definitely off-limits to grandchildren. However, to me it seemed to have been created just for my exploration. From my vantage point at the foot of the brown-painted stairs, I could stretch on tiptoes toward the faraway landing and barely see cracking linoleum, the peeping contents of stuffed storage boxes ("I wonder what could be in those?"), and a wall decorated with a picture of a recovering alcoholic at another addict's bedside. I was very certain that there were intriguing family secrets lying within those boxes, not to mention a great view out the bedroom windows. Who knew what other discoveries awaited at the top of the stairs?

The other mystery at my grandparents' house was a very different one. It was a simple table trivet that my grandmother had placed on the wall near the stairway, right above the phone table. Usually I resisted the temptation to climb the forbidden stairs; however, the ancient-looking black and red lettering of the trivet captivated me: "Today is the tomorrow you worried about yesterday."

I remember standing before the wall and gazing at the enigmatic words, mulling them over and over in my head, as I tried to solve the riddle about time. It was many years later when I finally understood the meaning of the adage. Maw Maw's trivet probably never held a hot casserole. Sometimes I have wondered why she chose to display it rather than use it for its intended purpose. But, as I learned when I was older, my grandmother had seen her share of worrisome yesterdays; perhaps she had personal reasons for hanging it on the wall in a prominent place.

Years passed, I grew up, and my grandparents eventually changed their address. The cousins' front porch became the property of a college fraternity, and someone else got to explore the upstairs. When my grandmother passed away in 1988 and all the many whatnots she had collected through the years were divided among her twenty grandchildren, her table trivet was the only object that I really wanted to own.

Today that trivet is on display in my kitchen. It reminds me that tomorrow's worries, as tempting as they are for me to dwell upon, are not meant for me to deal with today. On the other hand, the opportunity for intimacy with my Father is for the here and now.

Only in the present moment can I make the choice to live from my union with the One who lives outside both time and circumstance; I can't choose today for yesterday or for tomorrow. In this present place of abiding, I am a free explorer of the wonders of Jesus' eternal life that dwells inside me, a life which neither trial nor the passage of time can ever diminish or alter. I have no need to request permission to seek, and I need not fear that He will one day change His address. Rather than simplistic promises or fatalistic words about the inevitability of trouble, I have the unique reassurance that only Jesus has the authority to give: "I will never desert you, nor will I ever forsake you… [I am] the same yesterday and today and forever."

His is Life undaunted by life—now that's an even better riddle to ponder.

Related Verses:

Isaiah 40:31

Maw Maw's Trivet

Hebrews 13:5-8

Philippians 4:6-7

John 15:5

John 16:33

The Life of a Sugar Cane Stalk

L ouisiana's sugar industry has come a long way since Jesuit priests planted the first sugar cane in New Orleans in 1751. Those early planters could hardly have envisioned that Louisiana would become a major sugar producer, with over half a million acres in cultivation.

The Life of a Sugar Cane Stalk

Sugar cane is actually a grass with a much thicker stalk and much larger leaves than the grass in our yards. It is planted in August and September and grows through the year, most rapidly during the

Sugar mill

summer months, when it may grow over an inch a day. The cane is harvested from October through December, the period known as grinding season. The lush green sea of tall, swaying sugar cane awaiting harvest adds lovely texture to our flat landscape.

It's hard to believe that the end product of sugar cane cultivation is the minute white crystals in our sugar bowls. How does the sugar get from the stalk to the spoon? It isn't an easy road for the cane.

First, huge mechanical harvesters cut the cane tops and sever the cane at the base of the stalks. On the day after they are cut the leaves of the cut cane—comprising about 15% of the cane—are burned away, and large wagons transport the stalks to the mills. There a shredder washes and chops them into uniform pieces. Next, mills crush the cane to extract the raw juice. This cane juice is then purified, clarified, filtered, boiled, and crystallized into sugar.

What a process! Without the entire series of steps, though, none of us could have a sweet tooth. The sugar cane stalk is tough and woody, and without the grinding process the sap could never be obtained. Have you ever tasted a slice of fresh cane? Even after you've cut away the outer layer of the stalk, the cane is so fibrous that to extract the juice you really have to work hard at chewing!

God has put something sweet inside every believer—Christ in us, our hope of glory. He wants to "sweeten" others with the life of Christ through us, ministering to them His love and His grace. However, we have something else inside us—our flesh. The flesh is our self-life. It's our self-sufficiency and our "I-can-do-it-myself" attitude. It struggles against God's Spirit, and it prevents the life of Christ from "getting out," much as the outer stalk keeps the sweet cane juice inside the plant.

As long as we are living life from our own reserve of abilities and resources, the life of Jesus cannot be released to the world, and others will never taste His sweetness. That's why God must deal with our flesh. He must get it out of the way so His life can be released. God will allow crushing difficulties in our lives in order to strip us of our independence. This personal "grinding season" is designed to destroy our dependence on anything or anyone but Jesus and to make us turn to Him alone to find life and identity.

Jesus spoke highly of the woman who anointed him with costly perfume. What would have happened if she had brought the perfume to Jesus but had not broken the bottle to release its contents? There would have been no fragrance to fill the room. She had to break the outer vessel before the pleasant aroma could be released and the perfume could be used for its intended purpose.

If we are to fully experience and become conduits of the life of Jesus, then, like the stalk of sugar cane and the perfume bottle, our outer humanity must be broken as well. Though the process is far from painless, there is joy in the midst of the trials that He allows us to experience. We have the assurance from God that hope will not disappoint us, because the love of God has been poured out in our hearts through Jesus Christ. He is always present with us in all His sweetness, which He longs to pour out on others through us.

Related Verses:

Colossians 1:27

Mark 14:3

1 Peter 4:12

Romans 8:35-39

James 1:2-4

2 Corinthians 1:1-7

The Miracle Water of Abita Springs

One Louisiana town logo boasts that it is a place "where nature performs miracles." Abita Springs, a community in St. Tammany Parish that is home to about 2,000 citizens, got its name from an Indian phrase meaning "large settlement by the fountain," referring to the pure spring water in the area. In the 1800s, citizens of New Orleans in search of better health were sent

St. Augustine in His Study, by Vittore Carppacio, 1502

to Abita Springs to drink this water, which supposedly had curative effects.

Claims of the miraculous are often met with skepticism, but I appreciate the 4th century assessment of St. Augustine, who wrote, "Miracles are not contrary to nature, but only contrary to what we know about nature." His statement implies that we are able to comprehend only a small part of nature, because God alone understands His creation and is in fact above its laws.

Miracles are not relegated to human medicine. They happen around us all the time. God's infinite power makes miracles observable to me, and His infinite love allows me to behold them as delightfully confounding. I witness "impossibilities" all the time which challenge my comprehension but which I receive and enjoy nonetheless.

We were created with the ability to ask "why." But shouldn't we sometimes ask, "Why not?" Why must all occurrences be explicable? As created entities, do we have the right to demand an explanation of the inscrutable? Perhaps open-mouthed wonder is a more humble response to the miraculous.

The word miracle developed from the Latin word *miraculum*, meaning "object of wonder." Going further back, the word *miraculum* is believed to have originally come from words meaning "to wonder at" and "to smile or be astonished." Children universally feel surprise and pleasure at remarkable events that they did not anticipate. Perhaps the childlike faith to which Jesus Christ referred in the gospels includes the ability to simultaneously reason as an adult, believe by faith as a child, and experience joyful wonder as both.

Do you believe in a dynamic Creator who has gifted you with a greater ability to wonder than to understand? He allows us to exult in the inconceivable in spite of our limited comprehension of it. Because we are not the architect or the engineer of this world, our understanding of its operative laws is limited; however, we can still marvel at the miraculous without needing to know more than the simple fact that miracles do happen all around us every day—some of them in Abita Springs!

Related Verses:

> Acts 2:22
>
> Psalm 36:9
>
> Isaiah 25:1
>
> Isaiah 55:9
>
> Ephesians 1

The UCM Museum (Abita Mystery House) in Abita Springs

Marrow and Fatness

The unassuming crawfish is inextricably linked to Louisiana. Native Americans ate crawfish long before the arrival of Europeans and Acadians, and references in historical records prove that even the holes dug by the tiny crustacean left their effects. The *Western Gazetteer*, published in 1817, describes the surprising result of crawfish activity on the levees from New Orleans southward along the Mississippi River. "A vast quantity of water is continually oozing through the porous embankments, and in many places gushes through holes made by crawfish, which often increase so rapidly as to cause a breach in the levee."

A later Louisiana author mentioned crawfish in a more positive light. In 1840, Eliza Ripley, in her recollections of life in old New Orleans, recalled happy memories when "we children went crawfishing in the ditches" along Canal Street.

I've gone "crawfishing" several times with my family and friends, both along the Atchafalaya Basin levee and in the Airline Highway borrow pit. I never worried about the possibility of alligators or snakes intruding on our pleasant excursion, though I'm sure they were near, and the ensuing crawfish boil made the risks worthwhile.

But Louisiana crawfish boils are not an invention of this century. Lieutenant Colonel A.W. Hyatt, a New Orleans soldier during the Civil War, journaled that "Old [General] Kirby [Smith] has a little too much on his hands, taking care of three States…and at the same time watching over a bran [sic] new wife and going to pic-nics and blackberry and crawfish parties."

An account published in *The Historical Sketch Book and Guide to New Orleans and Environs,* published in 1885, bears witness to the nutritional value of the mudbug. The "high water" of 1884 left many people stranded and without access to food. When the floodwaters receded, there were found "twenty human beings in the one old rookery…completely surrounded by water, and without means to procure provisions. They had been living on crawfish for two days." Crawfish actually provided these flood victims with protein, calcium, iron, niacin, selenium, phosphorus, and vitamins A and B.

Besides being nutritious, crawfish have no carbohydrates and are low in saturated fats, in spite of the orange-yellow "fat" of the boiled crawfish, which contains much of the flavor. This substance is actually an organ called the hepatopancreas. Though some observers find repulsive the habit of eating the "fat" out of a crawfish head, diehards stand by their habit of rating the quality of a sack of boiled crawfish by how much of the matter they discover when they open the carapace.

The enjoyment of fat is not unique to Louisiana. Marrow, the fatty tissue inside animal bones, was in biblical times a nourishing delicacy that satiated a diner who sought a rich meal. A feast with marrow was considered lavish, meaning that it was a banquet filled with fatty items that left the eater stuffed and satisfied when he had finished his meal. Today science is proving the healing benefits of animal bone marrow when cooked down in bone broth.

Marrow and Fatness

God is into fatness and fullness. In Jeremiah, God proclaimed that He would saturate the souls of His priests with abundance, or fatness, of His goodness. The New Testament also speaks of fullness, referring to our being filled up through Christ to all the fullness of God.

In the 19th century, author Henry David Thoreau defended his decision to make his home in the wilderness in order to "live deep and suck out all the marrow of life." (*Walden; or, Life in the Woods*, 1854.) His use of that phrase makes me picture family and friends gathered around a table enjoying boiled crawfish with corn and potatoes. It's great to enjoy the wilds, but we don't have to live in isolation as Thoreau did in order to get all there is to get out of life. We have the Lifegiver

Himself living inside us. We can live with souls that are satiated with the marrow and fatness of God's goodness and grace.

The real feast isn't a plot of land on a lake, and it isn't even a crawfish boil. The feast is really Jesus. Let us say with the psalmist, "My soul is satisfied as with fatness" (Psalm 63:5), the rich marrow of His love.

Related Verses:

Isaiah 25:6

Jeremiah 31:14

Luke 1:53

Acts 13:52

Ephesians 3:19

Colossians 1:19

"Lost" Bread

One of my favorite breakfasts as a child was "lost" bread, otherwise known as *pain perdu,* or French toast. Before the appearance of sliced bread in grocery stores, a loaf of bread did not have the long shelf life it has today, so it quickly became stale, or "lost." In order not to waste this old bread, Louisiana mothers prepared it as lost bread.

The ingredients for lost bread include eggs, milk, sugar, and vanilla, which are combined to form a batter in which the bread is dipped and then pan-fried in either oil or butter. It is tasty eaten with butter and cinnamon sugar or with Steen's cane syrup on top, though many people enjoy it with powdered sugar or some other topping.

Once the battered slice of bread has been cooked, the original bread has been transformed into an entirely new dish that doesn't look, smell, or taste at all like dry, old bread. It now smells and tastes sweet and has a tender, moist texture. You could say that the old bread died and was reborn in the pan as French toast. It went into the batter as stale bread and came off the griddle as an entirely new breakfast item—delicious *pain perdu.*

What if we take a piece of dry bread and simply spread it with batter and served it on a plate uncooked? Would its identity be changed?

No, because it would still be stale bread, with only a raw coating on the surface. Something must happen to the stale bread if it is to become lost bread: it must be cooked. It must become completely different from the inside out.

The story of lost bread gives an illustration of what happens when a person becomes a Christian. All of us were born into this world as "stale" or "lost" human beings, incomplete and without the life of God. However, when we became Christians, we were baptized, or "dipped," into Jesus Christ. Just as the bread became identified with the batter by being immersed and saturated in it and then cooked, we identified with Jesus in His death, burial, and resurrection at the moment we believed in Him. He transformed us from the inside out, and we became new creatures. Jesus didn't make us better people; He gave us life that is altogether new and different—His own resurrection life!

A "batter" or coating of good behavior or law-keeping applied to our life will not make us holy or acceptable to God. What we need is not a changed nature but a completely new nature. And once a Christian, we need the very life of Jesus inside us to be able to live a life that pleases God, because it is impossible for us to do it on our own. Jesus was the only man who ever expressed God's holy nature in the flesh. He is still doing it today in believers who trust Him by faith to live His own life through them.

Lost bread would never be identified on a breakfast menu as "mouth-watering stale bread slices dipped in batter." Not many people would find that description appetizing! A menu would call the dish what it really is—lost bread, *pain perdu*, or French toast. The truth is that it's no longer stale bread.

"Lost" Bread

Let's remember the truth about who we are in Christ. God no longer calls us sinners, but rather saints. We have a new identity! By faith we have been transformed once and for all through the death, burial, and resurrection of Jesus Christ into new creations. Let your life reflect who you really are. And if you haven't tried it before, taste some lost bread and marvel at what stale bread can become when it gains a new identity.

Related Verses:

Colossians 2:12

2 Corinthians 5:17

Romans 6:4-11

Galatians 6:15

2 Timothy 1:9

The Better Part

Some people say that listening is a lost art, but my friend Jennie proves them all wrong. Jennie came home to Louisiana when she ended her career as a flight attendant. She has returned to her roots here in South Louisiana, and she tells me that she is learning to listen.

Jennie moved into a cottage right across the levee from Ole Man River himself. It seems that years of catching a few winks on a plane or in an airport lounge definitely didn't prepare her for retirement on the "silent" Mississippi River. Nighttime along the levee turned out to be anything but silent for Jennie. She heard the occasional blast of a tugboat or ship on the river, and she grew accustomed to the nocturnal noises of the Louisiana swamp—deep bullfrog croaks issuing from within woods alive with a chorus of crickets, katydids, and hoot owls. There were the creepy, human-sounding footfalls of armadillos shuffling through leaves around the house and the sounds that issued from beneath her bedroom floor as they burrowed in the earth and then, when startled, jumped into the air against the bottom of the house. And on her first night there were also imaginary sounds conjured up after we spent the afternoon playfully recounting tales of alligators and black bear that frequented the woods and swamp behind her cottage.

A Home on the Mississippi, by Currier and Ives, 1871, depicting Woodland Plantation, West Pointe à la Hache, Louisiana

It's amazing how acutely we can listen when we want to do so. But isn't it interesting how easy it is to not stop and listen? I have never counted the number of bird songs in my back yard. Do I know how many different sounds moving water makes? And a child's verbal tirade—what do I hear behind those words?

Listening is not simply a matter of the ears. The ears are only sensory organs; they don't interpret. They can receive sound waves, but they can't receive the message being sent. Listening is receiving with the heart what has been heard with the ear. It's "soaking up" sounds and all that they mean, to the exclusion of other distractions. It's Jennie quivering in her bed her first night on the river because she is taking in every sound she hears, or at least thinks she hears.

The gospel of Luke talks about a true listener. One day Jesus came to visit with his two friends, Martha and Mary. Upon Jesus' arrival, Martha was "distracted with all her preparations." Mary, on the other hand, was "seated at the Lord's feet, listening to His word."

Martha has had a lot of bad press for being occupied with service rather than a seat. Of course, service is a good thing. In every home there are things that must be accomplished. So what did Martha do that was so bad? Perhaps Martha's failure was not in what she did, but

Christ in the House of Mary and Martha, by Johannes Vermeer, circa 1655

rather in what she didn't do. Martha felt that her greatest need was to do for Jesus, when all the while He wanted her to receive what He had done for her. She was hearing Him, but was she really listening and receiving? Was her focus on her relationship with Jesus, or was it on the outcome of her service?

Could it be that at the end of the evening, when the porch light went out and Jesus said farewell to the women, Martha went to bed feeling that somehow she had missed out on something big? *I wonder what Jesus told Mary*, she might have thought. Martha could look back on Jesus' visit and say, "I served Jesus." Mary, on the other hand, was able to say, "I spent time with Jesus!" Which woman heard His heart? Mary really listened. And Jesus said that she had chosen the better part.

When it comes down to it, God doesn't need our service at all. It's the hearts of you and me and my friend Jennie that He desires. Perhaps sitting "at His feet" is not so much an issue of time and place—a certain spot or hour for a quiet time—as it is a matter of resting each moment in Jesus, whether we are busy or not.

Doesn't this kind of rest take the pressure to perform off of us? We find ourselves not worried about perfection in our service but rather relaxed in His gaze. As we listen to, receive from, and obey Him in total dependence upon Him, He lives through us.

Before Jesus died, He said that He was going to prepare a place for us. Certainly, He is preparing a home for us in heaven. But He has also prepared a place here and now for us, one of rest in Him, of seclusion from a noisy world filled with distraction and obligation.

When Jennie sits on her front porch across the highway from the levee, I hope she soaks in every bit of life going on about her. I hope that as the sun sets over Ole Man River she gets "holy goose bumps." As she glimpses the familiar silver ribbons of jets crisscrossing the Louisiana sky above the Mississippi River, I hope she savors every last sound and sight and smell of her once-again home, even if one of them might involve an alligator or a bear. And I pray that she and her friends, both new and old, will live at the feet of our Savior and Life, listening and allowing our hearts to hear Jesus.

Related Verses:

Luke 10:38-42

Mark 9:7

John 17:8

Acts 17:11

1 Corinthians 2:12

Hebrews 4:16

Mississippi River bridge in Baton Rouge

The Exotic Invader

Perhaps one of the most breathtaking sights in the Louisiana swamp is a blanket of bright green water hyacinths with their attractive lavender flowers. Unfortunately, the lovely water hyacinth is actually an invader to our wetlands.

In 1884, when the exotic-looking hyacinth was introduced from South America at the Cotton States Exposition in New Orleans, no one could have guessed that such a plant would one day be a nuisance. Water hyacinths keep light from getting to underwater plants for photosynthesis (www.lamer.lsu.edu, 2017). The plants die, reducing the amount of oxygen produced in the water. The loss of oxygen in turn affects animal life. This cycle of death and decay causes the waterway to be effectively choked to death. In addition, the decaying plant matter causes more sediment to build up on the floor of the waterway, which can eventually become like a bog.

Another problem is that hyacinths multiply prolifically, forming mats that clog waterways and sometimes make boating and fishing impossible. Boaters inadvertently transport pieces of the plant on their motors and trailers. The state of Louisiana budgets enormous resources just to try to control the spread of the water hyacinth.

The invasion of the water hyacinth proves that beauty can be deadly, a truth that Adam and Eve experienced firsthand in the Garden of Eden. Though their garden home included "every tree that is pleasing to the sight," they set their sights on the enticing fruit of the one tree that God had instructed them to avoid—the tree of the knowledge of good and evil.

Instead of eating from the Tree of Life (representing Jesus), which grew in the midst of the garden, they chose to act independently of their Creator. Eve's choice may have seemed innocuous to her at the time, but it had far-reaching consequences. It resulted in the entrance of sin and death into the world. Only Jesus' death and resurrection redeemed us from that wrong decision and gave us life.

Every day we face the same choice that Eve did. We can pursue our own path independently of God, or we can walk in surrender and dependence upon Jesus. Like the appealing bloom of the invasive hyacinth, the allure of a self-determined life is deceptive. It may appear exciting or fulfilling, but life lived apart from Jesus is not really living at all. We weren't created to go it alone in this world. God never meant for us to live the Christian life on our own. Only Jesus can live that life, and when we live dependently on Him, He lives it through us. We are then eating from the Tree of Life.

Related Verses:

Genesis 3:6-7

Romans 5:12

2 Corinthians 11:14

John 15:4

1 Thessalonians 5:22

In the Eye of the Storm

One of the realities of living along the coast of the Gulf of Mexico is the inevitability of at least a brush with a hurricane. You have probably witnessed an on-the-scene television meteorologist clinging to a railing in 100-mile-per-hour hurricane winds and pelting rain.

But the duration of a hurricane is not all wind and rain. The eye of the storm is eerily quiet, with clear skies and calm winds. You might

Hurricane Katrina, radar image showing the eye

In the Eye of the Storm

Gramercy sugar refinery after the hurricane of 1909

think you were done with the hurricane and could go about your business. However, if the eye of the storm is forecast to pass over your location, you'd better stay sheltered—you are about to get hit by the "other side" of the storm. High winds will shift to the opposite direction and will be at least as fierce as in the first half of the storm.

Sometimes it seems that life hits us with one "hurricane" after another. Just when things are looking up, and we think we see brighter days ahead, we are knocked over again. Even the mere prospect of another difficulty wears upon us.

When we go through a hard time, our own personal resources suddenly seem inadequate. Life feels topsy-turvy. But it is in the midst of hard times that we turn to God to be our stability and our security. We are forced to depend upon Jesus. We receive fresh insight into our own need to depend upon Him not only in trial, but in every moment of our lives.

If life seems to be a tempest to you, or if it is presenting you with a "new normal" that doesn't quite fit into your plans, cling to Jesus. Let Him be life to you. He will not let you go. He alone conquered the world and understands that we live with its frustrations, disappointments, disillusionments, and pain. As you endure the trial trusting in Him, He will prove to be what you need. He is the grace and truth of God in every moment and for every need.

Let Him envelop you so closely and intimately that you feel His arms about you rather than the shuddering of the storm. He is Lord in the storm.

Related Verses:

2 Thessalonians 3:16

James 1:12

1 Peter 1:6

Romans 8:18-25

The Spiderweb Wedding

Over a hundred years ago, the owner of a smaller plantation in St. Martin Parish, Charles Durand, hosted a unique double wedding for his two daughters. He wanted their marriage celebration to be an extravagant and unforgettable event, so he imported spiders from China and had them placed in the branches of the lengthy oak and pine alley leading up to his mansion. Within a few days, the spiders had spun their webs all along the pathway.

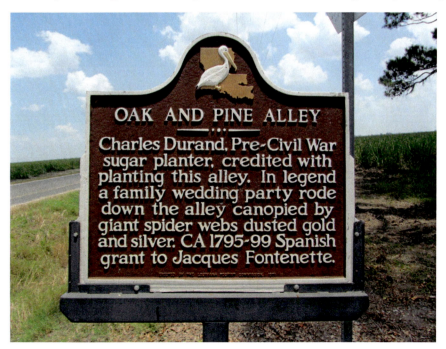

Lagniappe upon Lagniappe

Oak and Pine Alley, spring 2012

Then, shortly before the wedding was to take place, he had servants powder the entire line of trees with gold and silver dust. What an awe-inspiring sight the shimmering tree-lined path to the house must have been to the invitees, as their carriages drove down the long alley to the ceremony! Not surprisingly, the Durand spiderweb wedding has remained the subject of local lore to this day.

In 1955, another wedding was solemnized at Oak and Pine Alley. Two sisters—Charles Durand's great-great-granddaughters—staged their own double wedding, a re-enactment of the original spiderweb wedding. The celebration was part of the bicentennial commemorating the expulsion of the Acadians from Nova Scotia.

The arrival of guests at both weddings must have been quite a fashion spectacle, as they arrived in carriages or cars in their wedding finery. Such an extraordinary wedding demanded an extraordinary wardrobe! No guest would have dreamed of attending in everyday attire.

The idea of "grand dress for a grand occasion" is appropriate in many situations. However, when the question of the proper attire for New Testament worship is raised, this motto is not necessarily true.

Under the Old Covenant, the attire of the priesthood was carefully prescribed. According to Exodus 28, God commanded Moses to make specific holy garments "for glory and for beauty" for Aaron to wear as he served as a priest in the tabernacle. These garments were to be sewn of blue, purple, and scarlet material interwoven with gold threads. The breastpiece was studded with twelve precious stones set in gold.

In the establishment of the New Covenant, God changed the emphasis on clothing. Aaron's "holy attire" had been demanded under the Old Covenant. However, that covenant was only a shadow of the new one. Once Jesus made it possible for us to come into God's presence through His death, approaching God became an internal issue. Is Christ living inside of you? If you have received His gift of grace at the cross, then you are wearing "holy attire." You are wearing the righteousness of Christ.

The phrase "in holy attire" can also be translated "in the majesty of holiness." There is no one as majestic in holiness as Jesus Christ, and there is no fabric or clothing that is inherently holy or that will make our worship more acceptable to God. To believe that we can come to our Father simply on the basis of our appearance is to spurn His costly sacrifice: if our holiness could have been achieved on any other basis than the cross, would the Father have allowed His Son to suffer and die?

Aaron the High Priest, by an unknown artist, circa 1000

One day there will be a historic heavenly celebration. The bride (believers in Jesus) will be presented to the groom (Jesus). The bride will be dressed in her finest. Her bridal garment, though, will not be one that she has purchased or produced for herself. The wedding dress of the church of Jesus Christ will be the works that Jesus has done through us. Our wedding attire will be a gift from Him and not a result of our own labor. What a joyous celebration there will be at that marriage!

Though Mr. Durand obviously provided an unforgettable wedding celebration for his daughters, gold and silver dust can't compare to the extravagance that Jesus will lavish on His bride, the church, at the marriage of the Lamb. It will be part of heavenly lore for all eternity.

Related Verses:
Exodus 28:40

2 Chronicles 20:21

Psalm 96:9

Revelation 19:7-8

Ephesians 4:24

Lagniappe

The giving of *lagniappe* (pronounced [**lon**-yop]) is an old custom in Louisiana that endures to this day. *Lagniappe* is "a little something extra" that a proprietor gives to customers. For example, a storeowner might hand a free stick of candy to the client's child when he or she departs, saying, "Here's some *lagniappe* for you!" Though the French in Louisiana popularized the concept of *lagniappe*, the word itself originated with the Quechua Indians of the South American Andes and referred to something that was added or increased. When Spain took over the Incan empire, the Spanish acquired the expression and then brought it with them to Louisiana.

Mark Twain was familiar with the custom of offering *lagniappe*. In *Life on the Mississippi*, published in 1883, he wrote:

> We picked up one excellent word—a word worth travelling to New Orleans to get; a nice limber, expressive, handy word—'lagniappe.' They pronounce it lanny-yap. It is Spanish—so they said. We discovered it at the head of a column of odds and ends in the Picayune, the first day; heard twenty people use it the second; inquired what it meant the third; adopted it and got facility in swinging it the fourth. It has a restricted meaning, but I think the people spread it out a little when they choose. It is the equivalent of the thirteenth roll in a baker's dozen. It is something thrown in, gratis, for good measure.

Lagniappe

The idea of receiving a valuable gift at no cost to the taker began a long time before Twain picked up the word *lagniappe* and even before the Quechuas coined the term. Before Adam and Eve sinned in the garden and plummeted humanity into separation from God, the Father had already determined that He would *lagniappe* us with salvation through

From *Life on the Mississippi*, by Mark Twain, 1883

Lagniappe upon Lagniappe

His Son. He would initiate reconciliation with Himself and would freely offer forgiveness to us through the cross of Jesus. With Jesus' death, all we would have to do is receive His gift. The New Testament assures us that God's free gift to us is eternal life. All we need do is receive it.

But the Bible says that we have received more than salvation in Jesus. Not only did He pay for our sins and gain us access to heaven, but He has put His very own life inside of believers. We have received not just a little something extra, but rather grace upon grace, or as a Louisianan might say, "*lagniappe* upon *lagniappe*." Such an offer is like the invitation of a storeowner who says, "Well, I already gave you *lagniappe*, but here—you can every single treat in the store!"

Even though a kind retailer offers a delicious treat to a child, and even though there are no strings attached to the goodie, the youngster won't enjoy a single taste unless he first extends his hand and receives the candy as his own. Imagine the joy of the storeowner as he sees a young customer reach out to receive his gift. Then imagine joy on the face of God as we receive from Him what He delights to give us and what we could never earn. He rejoices when we accept from Him all that He offers us for free—nothing less than forgiveness and the holy resurrection life of Jesus inside us.

But how can we as humans contain the life of God? Why would a holy God desire to share His life with us? How can the flawless life of Jesus live inside of us imperfect beings?

God's solution to our dilemma was twofold. First, He sent His Son to pay for our wrongdoing. Then, in addition, He crucified our old self on the cross with Jesus, buried us with Him, and then raised us with Him to life—His resurrection life. We were forgiven and cleansed in order that we might become containers of Jesus' holy life! We are now alive to God and His life in us is our strength and our hope of glory.

This idea seems too good to be true. Most believers rejoice in the forgiveness aspect of the cross; however, the second part—the fact that Jesus wants to do holy living for us, in us, and through us—is the "*lagniappe* upon *lagniappe*" of the New Testament. He forgives us, and then He lives the Christian life for us and in us and through us!

Twain was not referring to the grace of God when he wrote about the word *lagniappe*, but his description still fits. *Gratis* means "free of charge" and is related to the word *grace*! As creator of the idea that it's more blessed to give than to receive, God was the original benefactor of *lagniappe*. His children freely receive His grace in layer upon layer, both unto salvation and through the life of His Son lived within us.

Related Verses:

John 1:16

Romans 3:23-24

Romans 6:23

Galatians 2:20

Ephesians 1:6

Ephesians 2:6

A Note to the Reader

Thanks for reading my book! I welcome your response to its message. You can email me or purchase copies at www.pammussobraud.com.

Made in the USA
San Bernardino, CA
22 April 2017

CPSIA information can be obtained
at www.ICGtesting.com
Printed in the USA
BVHW04s2052210718
522289BV00022B/793/P